Appolina Anteater and her Amazing Animal Friends !

SEAN COOPER

DEDICATION

For Lisa

ACKNOWLEDGMENTS

A very special mention to Mr. Simon Griffiths, the Headmaster at Lindens Primary School in Walsall.

Also to his talented pupils who provided the illustrations, which inspired the gifted Irana Nasrin to transform into the Wonderful images inside this book.

Appolina Anteater lives in deep Peru

She loves to dance to Samba

Do you like dancing too?

She likes to swing

She likes to sway

As she hoovers up the ants

But most of all she loves to boogie

In her big bright purple pants!

Berniece the Butterfly floats from leaf to leaf

She used to be a Caterpillar

But then she found belief

She sprouted wings so glorious and true

Now she flutters around your garden

To stop you feeling blue.

Christopher the Crocodile always wears a bright white smile

He likes to show his gnashers off

As he swims along the Nile

He pushes off the sun baked bank

With his tail swishing to and thro

His ancestors ruled Egypt

Long before the first Pharaoh!

Daisy is a Dingo from a pack of ten

She throws a rodent on the barbie

And eats it in her den

It's nice enough but tough to chew

This makes Daisy feel a little blue

So to make her feel jolly

She eats a lovely lizard lolly!

The real Queen of Africa is in no way silly

A glorious strong elephant whose Mother named her Lily

She flaps gigantic ears to cool down in the heat

Or sprays water high into the air

While she paddles with her feet

Lily tramples through the forest pulling up big trees

But if she ever spies a little mouse

She trembles at the knees!

Freddy is a cunning fox that comes out late at night

He trots through towns and cities under the moonlight

His wife she is a vixen her names Lisa Marie

She would like to prowl with Freddy but is busy cooking tea

They have a cub his name is Will who stole a chicken from a coop

But Lisa is not angry she puts it in her soup!

Gerrard is a gibbon that swings from tree to tree

He likes to show his bottom off to folk like you and me!

Gerrard loves bananas when it is time for lunch

He sometimes scoffs so many he eats them by the bunch!

He has them green

he has them yellow

Gerrard is a hungry fellow.

Harry is a hedgehog that lives under a bush

He roams around my garden and never seems to rush

For fifteen million years they have lived upon the earth!

Searching out yummy insects

Harry shows his worth

But when the nights draw in and it is chilly for our mate

He finds a nice warm haven a place to hibernate.

Iggy the Iguana is a real winner

He escapes from pesky predators by being a super swimmer

His eyesight is amazing he can spot lunch from afar

And when he spies that tasty treat

He really starts to move his feet!

Then for fun he plunges in the pool

Iggy is so super cool!

A Jaguar prowls through the glade

Hunting supper her name is Jade

Her bite is more powerful

Than that of a lion!

An awesome leap brings her prey down crying!

Do you know that Jade is an excellent swimmer?

And if she fancies a change from gazelle for dinner

She can hunt some fish but can't have chips!

So she will take a drink from the watering hole

Ah that's better long and cool refreshing sips.

Kitty is a kangaroo Australian and proud

She can leap and jump so far

If you saw her you would gasp out loud!

She carries her son in a pouch

His name? Well that is Joey

He will soon loosen the apron string

And take up boxing in the ring!

Lynette is a Lizard who hails from New Orleans

She likes to eat some bugs but would prefer baked beans!

Her skin is rough and scaly

Her face is looking old

She has a best friend from across the pond

A slimy little Toad.

Millie is a little mouse blessed with special gifts

She loves to play the bass guitar and listen to The Smiths!

She wears a leather jacket and nails the rock chick look

And likes to nibble on some cheese

She finds some oh what luck!

Nobby is a newt of distinguished repute

He sports a monocle and waistcoat topped with a top hat

It makes him look so dapper

He is happy about that!

He feeds on insects' snails and slugs and any other little bugs

If you search by lake or stream

You cannot miss him, he is bright green!

Nobby loves the suns warm rays

But as the evening turns to night

He goes to bed let's say goodnight.

Olly is an octopus he swims amongst the rays

But when he is not swimming he likes to spend his days

By pulling on his roller skates and skating at the rink

But if he gets a fright or scare he squirts a little ink!

Eight tentacles with skates he knows how to impress his mates!

But most of all he loves George his brother

Dad Jim and Claire his Mother.

Pongo the pig is feeding in his sty

Munch! Munch!

Crunch! Crunch!

And then it's time to lie

But first he will roll around the mud

He loves this, it's great fun!

And then it's time to snooze in the midday sun

Pongo has a lovely dream where pigs really do fly

A propeller on his curly tail takes him to the sky!

Queenie is a quail delicate and small

She used to live in Japan

Just ten centimetres tall!

Queenie likes barley, wheat and fruit

She also likes to play the flute

She likes to blast a screechy tune

To scare away hungry raccoon!

Ricky is a young Raccoon who lives out the back

His fur is mainly grey in colour but he wears a mask of black

It makes him look like Zorro who was handy with a sword

Ricky plays swashbuckling games

It stops him getting bored!

Sally is a seahorse who lives under the sea

She glides around the coral moving gracefully

On Saturday she will have to chase if she wants to win the race!

All the fish will be there to see

The fantastic!

Amazing!

Seahorse Derby!

Toby is a turtle who hatched upon a beach

He doesn't know his role in life

He thinks that he will teach

He wears a mortarboard neat upon his head

Lecturing young turtles until it's time for bed.

Ugho the umbrella bird lives high in a tree

He likes to hop from branch to branch and gobble frogs for tea!

The Amazonian rainforest is his natural habitat

But when torrential rain will fall

He does not need to wear a hat

He simply opens his large umbrella

For Ugho is a clever fella!

Vicky is a viper from the Cornish coast

She has a nasty bite when she is provoked!

She slithers and slides spits and hisses too!

I don't trust her one bit

I mean come on would you?

She lies upon the cliff top worshipping the sun

So please do not disturb

Her bite is not much fun!

Morrissey and Marr are brothers strong and true

Proud wolves from a loving pack

With wolf cubs one and two

The cubs are Andy and Mikey J

And it's their favourite time of day

For they are playing hide and seek

With small white plastic squeaky sheep!

Here is Xavier the x-ray fish wearing x-ray specs!

He has a yellow dorsal fin and swims through old shipwrecks

He spies a wooden treasure chest upon a broken deck

And is able to see inside with his amazing x-ray tech!

It's full of golden coins all sparkling just like new!

But there are no shops to be found down in the ocean blue!

So he swishes his tail

Determined he proceeds'

To explore a little more amongst the flowing reeds.

Yippitee yak wears her brand new mac

But surely there's no rain upon this sun baked plain?

Ah she sees Lily the elephant sucking up water

To cool down Nathalie her baby daughter

But the water flies everywhere!

Smart Yippitee with your new rainwear!

Now she can stay nice and dry

As she watches wildlife passing by.

Zack he is a zebra with stripes of black and white

He dreams of being a racehorse and run with all his might

Imagine if his dream came true!

Carrying his jockey in claret and blue

Zack thunders past the winning post

And celebrates with tea and toast!

www.ingramcontent.com/pod-product-compliance
Lightning Source LLC
LaVergne TN
LVHW072052070426
835508LV00002B/57